SO-DUV-610

HOW TO DETECT ALTERED & COUNTERFEIT
COINS
AND
PAPER MONEY

BY
BERT
HARSHE

ALTERED

GENUINE

SIXTH EDITION

HOUSE OF COLLECTIBLES, ORLANDO, FLORIDA

CJ
1832
.H38
1978

NATURAL HISTORY
library
ANGELES COUNTY

© 1978 by ANCO
Florence, Alabama

All rights reserved. No part of this book may be reproduced or utilized in any form or by any means, electronic or mechanical, including photocopying, recording, or by any information storage and retrieval system, without permission in writing from the Publisher.

Address all correspondence to the: House of Collectibles, Inc.
771 Kirkman Road
Suite 100
Orlando, FL 32811

Printed in the United States of America

Library of Congress Catalog Card Number: 78-61860

ISBN: 0-87637-104-7

INTRODUCTION

With the tremendous growth of the Numismatic hobby and a corresponding increase in altered coins, this booklet on how to identify altered coins should be a valuable reference especially for the beginning collector.

For some unknown reason, the attitude in most reference works seems to be that a few words of caution are sufficient to inform the collecting public about altered coins, as a result the uninformed collector is the one who pays.

We have attempted to give the collector a ready reference illustrating and describing coins frequently altered, with a genuine for comparison.

I don't mean to give the impression that coin collectors and dealers are all dishonest; by and large most are honest, and will not knowingly sell an altered coin; however, as in other fields we have our "bad apples."

I wish to thank the people who helped make this book possible, especially John Tkach, Harold N. Dally, Muray Pearce, Willard Riggs and Roger Bender.

Thanks to author Jack Tod and Lee Hewitt of "Numismatic Scrapbook" for the study of the 1909-S and 1909S V.D.B. Lincoln cents.

This edition includes a section on Counterfeit Mint Errors by Alan Herbert, author of "The Odd Corner" column which appears in "Numismatic News Weekly."

Bert Harsche

TABLE OF CONTENTS

GENERAL INFORMATION

The most common methods used in altering coins are:

Removing Metal, some examples are:

1834 half cent altered to 1831, 1874 Indian cent altered to 1871, 1940s cent altered to 1910s, 1941 D or S cent altered to 1911 D or S, 1942 D or S cent altered to 1912 D or S, 1944 D or S cent altered to 1914 D or S, 1930 D or S or 1936 D or S altered to 1931 D or S (some check for either), 1938 P or D cent altered to 1933 P or D, 1948 P D or S cent altered to 1943 P D or S copper cent, 1924 P or D dime altered to 1921 P or D, 1934 D dime altered to 1931 D, 1928 S quarter altered to 1923 S etc.

Removing existing mint marks on coins where the "P" mint coin is worth considerably more than the branch mint coin. Some coins to watch are the 1922 P cent, 1960 small date cent, barber halves of 1913, 1914, 1915, 1895 silver dollar, 1928 silver dollar, 1899 dollar, 1863 5 dollar gold, 1865 5 dollar gold, 1869 5 dollar gold, 1872 5 Denver gold, 1875 5 dollar gold, 1877 5 dollar gold, 1887 5 Denver gold, 1858 10 dollar gold, etc.

Examine the area of mint mark for evidence of tooling and buffing. On buffed coins the detail around the removed mint mark will be indistinct or blurred.

On an altered coin the field where the mint mark was removed is often not level. You will see a slight depression by holding the coin at an angle.

Shaving Blob Mint Marks

Some examples of this are:

1912 D Liberty nickel altered to 1912 S, 1916 S dime altered to 1916 D, 1909 D $5.00 gold altered to 1909-O.

See— 1912 S nickel, 16 D dime.

Splitting Coins

Examine coins with the mint mark on the reverse for evidence of split rim, especially nickels as they do not have a reeded rim.

A plain obverse and a mint marked reverse are planed down and the halves are soldered together.

Coins with a reeded rim are usually split by hollowing out a coin then reducing the size and thickness of another so that the reduced half fits into the hollowed out portion and soldered into position.

See 1950-D Jefferson Nickel.

Punched Mint Marks

A mint mark is punched on a plain coin and the metal around the mint mark is removed so the mint mark appears to be raised above the field.

Hold the coin at eye level and compare the height of the mint mark with detail around it.

Examine the area on the opposite side of the mint mark for a flat spot or a slight bulge.

Note: On the Indian head 2½ dollar gold and 5 dollar gold the mint mark is the highest point on the coin as the design is incuse.

Another method is to raise metal on a plain coin by drilling a hole into the coin on the opposite side of the mint mark until the remaining metal is very thin.

The remaining metal is then pushed up to form the raised mint mark and the hole is filled in.

Examine the area on the opposite side of the mint mark for evidence of the filling and buffing.

Soldered or Glued Mint Marks

Compare the size, shape and position of the mint mark with a genuine coin or photo of a genuine (the position will vary on the genuine).

Hold the coin at eye level and compare the height of the mint mark with other detail around it, also compare with other coins of the series to become familiar with the height, shape, and position of the mint marks.

Examine the base of the mint mark for the seam; you will need a good glass to see the thin line.

On silver coins look for evidence of removal of excess silver solder.

To Expose Glued Mint Marks

Treat the mint mark area with acetone (a solvent available at your drug store). This will not hurt a genuine, but after the test you should relubricate the coin with "care," oil or whatever you use to avoid corrosion on your coins.

Apply the acetone with a dropper or dunk the piece in acetone. After several minutes carefully push the mint mark with your fingernail. If it is a glued mint mark it will fall off.

Altering Varieties

1864 Bronze Cent altered to 1864 "L" or pointed bust variety by shaving the point of the bust on the blunt bust variety. See page 9.

1937 D Buffalo Nickel altered to 1937 D 3 leg by removing the leg. See page 20.

1942 Dime altered to 1941/42 dime by soldering a 1 over the "2" of a 1942 P dime. See page 25.

Fantasy Coins

Coins are altered to create dates and mint marks never minted, some examples are:

1940 D cent altered to 1910 D, 1945 P D or S Mercury dime altered to 1915 P D or S, 1945 P D or S Walking Liberty half dollar altered to 1915 P D or S, 1938 D Buffalo nickel altered to 1933 D, etc.

Polished Uncirculated or Proof?

Uncirculated coins are sometimes buffed or plated so that they appear to be proof.

A genuine proof coin will have a mirror surface that will reflect an image, sharp hair lines and detail.

An uncirculated coin has frosty luster and the small detail such as the steps on the Jefferson nickel are often lost.

A proof is struck with polished dies on hand picked planchets.

Examine all proof coins offered. You wouldn't buy an 1909S VDB without looking at it, would you?

Beware of dark areas around date or mint marks as this could hide solder marks or evidence of tampering.

I have illustrated rather crude copies of the altered coins to make the alteration more distinct in the photographs. You will see altered coins that show very little evidence of tampering, so examine them carefully. Remember that the coins are illustrated several times their actual size.

Use of Acid

Chemically pure (C.P.) nitric acid is used in the alteration of coins for several reasons. The first is the use of the acid to remove a genuine mint mark from another coin. A genuine mint mark is taken from a coin that has been cut or ground down near the area of the mint mark. The acid is applied to complete getting the mint mark by eating away the material left in the mint mark area. The result is a clean mint mark that can now be used to alter another coin.

Acid etch is also responsible for dots, overdates, flagpoles or other added attractions on coins.

On copper and nickel coins C. P. nitric acid is used full strength. If the acid is used with water the etching process is slower with a rough appearance left on the surface of the coin.

To produce a dot or whatever on any of these pieces a material that can not be eaten away by the acid must be used. This is normally something similar to asphalt paint. The dot is painted on the coin to be altered in the exact position and of the exact size as the genuine. The acid is applied to the complete surface of the coin and rubbed down so the surface of the coin will receive an even etch. After several applications the asphalt paint is removed and the results will be a dot in the right place on the altered coin.

Silver coins that require this same treatment will be etched with a solution of one part C. P. nitric acid, two parts of water and some tri-sodium phosphite.

Acid etch will still leave the mint marks or digits with rounded base. A genuine coin will have features that have a square base and this squarness can not be easily produced by acid etch or photo engraving.

A good magnifying glass is a must if you collect coins.
Never buy an altered coin, not even as a filler.

GENUINE

1. The center of the letter "O" in the word "of" is not rounded on the genuine 1856 Flying Eagle.

2. The letters "A" and "M" in "America" are connected by an uneven line on the genuine 1856 Flying Eagle.

3. Draw an imaginary line down the left side of the number "5." The line will point to the center of the ball on the tail of the number "5."

1858 LARGE LETTER FLYING EAGLE ALTERED TO 1856

ALTERED

1. On the coin altered from the 1858 large letter Flying Eagle, the center of the letter "O" in the word "of" is rounded.

2. The line connecting the letters "A" and "M" in the word "America" is straight, level with the bottom of the letters.

3. Draw an imaginary line down the left side of the number "5"; the line will point to the left of the ball on the tail of the number "5."

1799 LARGE CENT

A genuine 1799 Large Cent can be identified by a chip or lump on the reverse between the letter "E" in "One" and the "T" in "Cent." Examine date and chip on reverse for evidence of tampering.

1804 Large Cent

The genuine 1804 Large Cent can be identified in the following way:

On the genuine 1804 the "O" (zero) in the date is opposite the letter "O" in the word "of" on the reverse. Examine rim for evidence of split rim. Examine date for evidence of tampering.

1864 ALTERED TO 1864 L OR POINTED BUST VARIETY

GENUINE

The blunt bust of an 1864 is shaved to appear to be the 1864-L or pointed bust variety. The letter "L" must be visible to be worth the premium listed.

Many collectors don't know where the "L" is located. Learn to find it, the "L" is on all Indian cents after 1864. See the "L" illustrated above.

1874 INDIANHEAD CENT ALTERED TO 1871 INDIANHEAD CENT

GENUINE　　　　　　　　　　　**ALTERED**

Draw an imaginary line under the date, or use a piece of paper with a straight edge.

1. On the 1871, only the "8" and the "7" in the date will touch the line.

2. The date on the altered 1874 is level so all the numbers will touch the line.

Note: compare the top of the last "1" in the date of the genuine with the altered 1874.

1874-75-76-78 INDIAN CENT ALTERED TO 1877

GENUINE   ALTERED

On the 1873, 74, 75, 76, 78 the last number is removed and a 7 is glued in place.

Compare with the genuine 1877 illustrated for alignment of numbers in date, thickness of tops of 7's, and slant of the back side of the 7's.

To be genuine the numbers must match the photo of the genuine exactly. I have never seen a genuine using different date punches.

If you have a suspect coin, treat the date with acetone.

1908 AND 1909 INDIAN CENTS ALTERED TO 1908S AND 1909-S GLUED MINT MARKS

GENUINE

The 1908S and 1909S Indian cents I have seen have all had the style of "S" mint mark illustrated, larger than the early Lincoln cent mint marks.

If the mint mark does not match the one illustrated, examine the base for a seam and treat with acetone.

Beware of split 1909 plain with 1908 S reverse. See 1959 D nickel.

ALTERED 1909 S VDB

Altered 1909S VDBS are made in the following ways:

1. Combining a 1909-S obverse with a 1909 V.D.B. reverse by milling down the two coins and sweating together. Usually copper-flash plated and then rebrowned. Very difficult to detect. Becoming less predominant now that the price of 1909-S is high and with other methods explained below being used.

2. Combining a 1909-S obverse with 1909 V.D.B. reverse by inlaying the planed down V.D.B. reverse into a bored out 1909-S obverse. Hard to detect if copper-flash plated and then rebrowned.

3. Relief-etching a V.D.B. on the reverse of a regular 1909-S. Usually easy to detect with a magnifying glass by comparing with genuine piece.

4. Altering third numeral of 1939 S to a zero and then combining with V.D.B. reverse with one of the above methods.

5. Altering third numeral of 1929 S and matching to V.D.B. reverse. Usually detected by uneven field in date area. All numerals in date may not appear equal in height.

6. Punched-up S mint mark on milled 1909 obverse and mated to V.D.B. reverse. Detectible by mint mark position and inspection of mint mark.

7. Die struck coins made on spark erosion dies. Detectable in "new" pieces by grain structure (similar to sandblast proof), color, and minute detail. Would be virtually impossible to detect in any grades below XF if wear and color were simulated and genuine blank planchets were used. At this writing no authenticated pieces produced by spark erosion have been reported.

8. Soldered on S mint mark on regular 1909 V.D.B. Detectable with strong magnifier on "older models." Would be difficult to detect if piece given copper-flash and then rebrowned.

9. Glued on S mint mark. The S glued on regular 1909 V.D.B. with resin glue. If proper 1909 V.D.B. reverse type was used and if position and tilt of mint mark is precise, these extremely skillful fakes are virtually impossible to detect by inspection alone (even under strong magnification). Test is to dissolve the resin glue with acetone and S will come off.

10. Cast coins. Generally poor quality. However, pieces produced by centrifugal casting can be of good quality. A valuable tool in their detection is a micrometer and fine balance scale to weigh coins in grains. Castings are under weight and slightly undersized.

To expose these fakes first examine the reverse. There are eight stages of die imperfection on the plain V.D.B. reverse working dies relating to the V.D.B. as follows:

Various graduations of these eight varieties exist, of course. However, all 1909S V.D.B. reverses that I have seen had the type one reverse with all periods prominent. Only a small percentage of the 1909 P V.D.B. are type one. Make certain the suspect coin has all periods prominent.

No. 1 — V.D.B.

No. 2 — V.D.B

No. 3 — V.D B.

No. 4 — V D.B.

No. 5 — V.D B

No. 6 — V D.B

No. 7 — V D B.

No. 8 — V D B

Examine the position of the S mint mark. There were three working dies used for the 1909 S V.D.B. obverse. These are 1 high left, 2 high right, and 3 low right. See the photos of date elements.

The No. 1 — high left, tilts to right a great deal.

The No. 2 — high right tilts to right a moderate amount.

The No. 3 — low right is nearly vertical.

Not only must the mint mark be in one of these exact three positions, but it must also have the proper amount of clockwise tilt.

Examine the size and shape of the mint mark. The type of S on the 1909S V.D.B. is peculiar to the early S Lincolns in that the middle bar is much fatter than the top and bottom bar joining the serifs. This is less pronounced on pieces where the S has had some wear (below VF or so). On some pieces from the No. 1 and No. 3 dies, the upper open area in the S appears to be partly filled in.

Examine the line of cleavage between the attached S and the field of the coin. On the fakes, this juncture is a sharp angle. On some of the fakes, the line of cleavage at the field surface does not exactly follow the outline of the S at the open areas of the letter, especially on the left hand side. On some fakes, the S has been shaved down so thin that one or both of the serifs has been inadvertently bent out of normal alignment.

A good glass is necessary to detect the flaws noted.

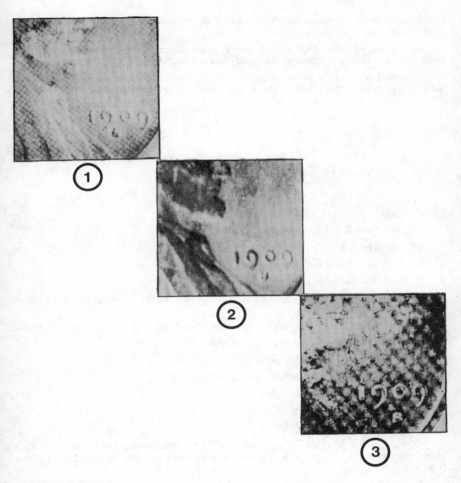

Additional Clues

A variety of die deterioration of the No. 3 die exists wherein there was die erosion in the area of the mint mark and along the rim near the date and under the bust. This makes these areas appear grainy as on many of the S mint coins in the mid 1920's (especially 1924S). If the piece is a No. 3 low right mint mark and has this feature, it is genuine.

It is well known that some 1909-S V.D.B. pieces exist with faint V.D.B. initials (faintest at the bottom of the letters). These coins come from die No. 3 LR but not all coins from No. 3 LR have the faint V.D.B. The P V.D.B. coins also occur with faint V.D.B., so if the suspect S-V.D.B. has a faint V.D.B. make certain it is from die No. 3.

If the coin is held in a reflecting light at a slight angle to the eye and it appears that the mint mark is slightly higher than the date it may be spurious. On genuine pieces the S is not higher than the date and the S on die No. 3 may appear to be a slight depression.

13

If you wish to come to the moment of truth on coins you own, treat the mint mark area with the acetone.

Apply the acetone with a dropper or swab. After several minutes, carefully push the mint mark, if it is a glued mint mark it will fall off.

This will not hurt a genuine piece, but after the test you should relubricate with "care" or whatever you use to avoid corrosion on your bronze coins.

1909 S CENTS

1909 s cents

Altered 1909 S are made in the following ways:

1. Glued mint marks.
2. Relief etching S minting mark.
3. Cast and die struck phonies.

The fake 1909-S cents are harder to detect because there are less clues (no VDB initials on reverse).

A total of six obverse dies were used for the 1909 S cents as pictured here:

Die No. 1—high left, the same as 1909-S V.D.B.

Die No. 2—high right, the same as 1909-S V.D.B.

Die No. 3—high right further right than No. 2.

Die No. 4—medium high right.

Die No. 5—low, far right.

Die No. 6—far low, far right.

Compare the position of the suspect 1909S mint mark with pictures. Also note other clues relating to the line of cleavage between the attached S and the field of the coin.

I would recommend that a detailed examination of each 1909S, 1909S V.D.B., 1914D, and 1931S be made.

Before purchasing one of these dates, treat the mint mark with acetone if visual inspection shows suspicion of a spurious piece.

1919-S ALTERED TO 1909-S CENT

This is done on a very poor coin much like the 1918 D cent altered to 1914 D.

14

1918-D CENT ALTERED TO 1914 D

ALTERED

A badly worn 1918 D cent is altered to a 1914 D cent by simply shaving the shadow of the "8" so it appears to be a four.

Examine the area around the "4" for evidence of tampering, also examine the shoulder for the VDB or for evidence of its removal.

1944 D CENT ALTERED TO 1914 D

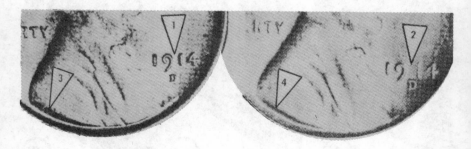

GENUINE   **ALTERED**

1. The genuine 1914 D cent has the numbers in the date evenly spaced.
2. The altered 1944 D cent has a wide space between the "9" and the second "1."
3. A genuine 1914 D does not have the initials VDB under the shoulder.
4. The altered date 1944 D may have the initials VDB on the shoulder, but this test is not conclusive as the VDB can be removed.

I have seen coins where the third number was entirely removed and a "1" glued between the "9" and "4" properly spaced. I have also seen a 1934 D altered to a 1914 D by the method described above.

This check will identify 1910 S, 1911 S, 1912 S, 1914 S, and 1915 S Lincoln cents.

16

1914 P CENT ALTERED TO 1914 D

1. See 1909 for punched mint mark and glued mint mark.

1922 D CENT ALTERED TO 1922 P

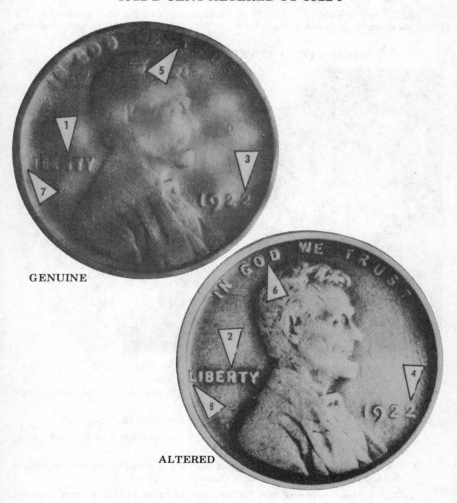

GENUINE

ALTERED

1. On a genuine 1922 P, the "R" in Liberty is mushy or blurred.
2. On an altered 1922 D the "R" is strong.

17

3. On a genuine 1922 P, the last "2" in date is weak and the tail is flattened.

4. On the altered 22D, the date will be evenly struck.

5. On the genuine the words "In God We" are blurred and the first "T" in the word "Trust" is a strong or clear strike.

6. The motto on the altered 22 is a strong even strike.

7. The letter "L" in "Liberty" is run into the rim on the genuine.

8. The "L" in "Liberty" does not touch the rim on the altered.

NOTE: Some weak "D" 22 D cents have some of the characteristics of a plain, so examine the area of the mint mark for evidence of buffing or tampering.

1930 S OR D ALTERED TO 1931 S OR D

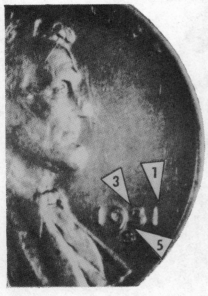
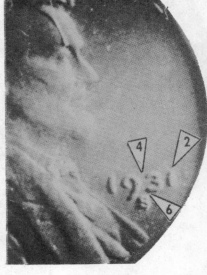

GENUINE   ALTERED

1. On a genuine 1931 S cent, the last "1" in the date is the same length as the first one.

2. On an altered 1936 S, the last "1" is shorter than the first "1."

3. On a genuine 1931 S, the top of the "3" is rounded and the end curves down.

4. On an altered 1936 S, the top of the "3" is straight; beware of tooling the top end to make it appear to curve.

5. The bottom curve of the "3" on the genuine 1931 S is long, pointed, and curves up close to the number "9."

6. On the altered 1936 S, the bottom of the "3" is short and does not curve as much as the genuine.

ALTERED 1931S CENT

Glued Mint Marks

Beware! I have seen 1931 S cents with mint marks attached so skillfully and so perfectly positioned that it was impossible with a strong glass to detect any abnormality whatsoever.

Nevertheless, application of some acetone caused the S to fall off the coin.

Examine all 1931-S cents very carefully. If permission is obtained treat the mint mark with acetone; if not, beware.

1938 D CENT ALTERED TO 1933 D

GENUINE

ALTERED

1. The numbers in the date of the genuine 1933 D cent are evenly spaced.

2. The space between the two "3's" is too wide on the altered 1938D.

NOTE: Compare the last three of the genuine with the last "3" of the altered coin. The width of the "3" on the genuine is greater.

1948 PDS ALTERED TO 1943 CENT

GENUINE   ALTERED

1. On genuine 1943 cent, the tail of the "3" is lower than the rest of the date.

2. On an altered 1948, the bottom or tail of the "3" is not lower than the rest of the date.

NOTE: 1943 steel cents are sometimes copper plated; a magnet will pick up a copper plated coin but not a genuine cent.

1960D SMALL DATE ALTERED TO 60P SMALL DATE

GENUINE   ALTERED

Examine the area of the mint mark for scratches or other evidence of tooling; hold the coin at eye level to see if there is a depression under the date.

If you have a suspect coin compare the weight with a cent showing the same amount of wear. The altered coin will weigh less.

Additional clues indicating removed mint marks are a highly polished depression and rounded bottom on the number "9."

1910 LIBERTY NICKEL ALTERED TO A 1913 LIBERTY NICKEL

GENUINE

ALTERED

The center of the "0" in date of 1910 is filled with metal, two holes are drilled to resemble the center of a "3," then the front is shaved to open the "3." Finally, the back is shaved. Examine the area described for evidence of altering.

NOTE: There are no 1913 Liberty Nickels in circulation or "lost." The 1913 is also manufactured from 1903 or 1908 Liberty Nickels.

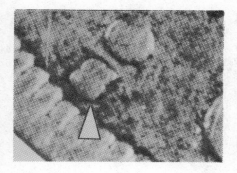

GENUINE

ALTERED

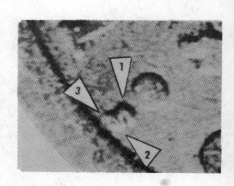

A blob "D" mint mark is shaved to resemble an "S." To accomplish this:

1. The upper left corner of the "D" mint mark is rounded.

2. The upper front is shaved.

3. The lower reverse is altered, the blob now appears to be an "S." A comparison with the genuine will show that it is not.

Examine the areas described for evidence of altering.

1956 D OR 1959 D JEFFERSON NICKEL ALTERED TO 1950 D

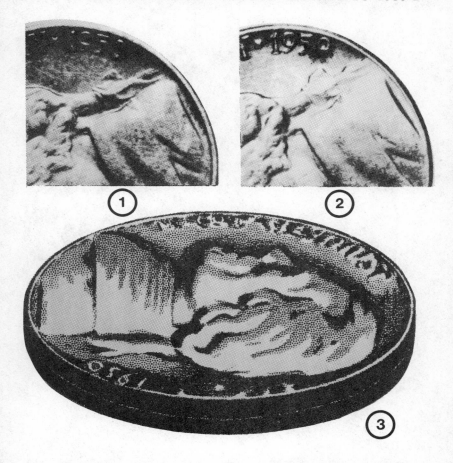

1. On genuine 1950 D nickel, the numbers in date are of the same size.

2. On the altered 1956 D or 1959 D, the "0" in the date is very small.

3. Beware of split coins. Example: a 1950 plain obverse and a "D" mint reverse.

This evidence could be on the rim as illustrated on the obverse or reverse next to the rim.

Those with evidence of tampering on the obverse or reverse are made by hollowing out a nickel and reducing the size and thickness of another nickel so that it fits inside the hollowed out portion, then soldered into position.

Beware of glued mint marks.

I have heard of a 1958 D being altered to a 50 D by punching out the center of the number "8." Inspection of the number should expose these fakes. If the zero in the date does not match the illustration of the genuine it is fake.

GENUINE

1. The entire buffalo is smaller on the genuine 3-leg; this can be seen with the naked eye.

2. On the altered 1937 D, the buffalo is larger.

3. The hind legs on the genuine 3-leg are narrow and not fully rounded which gives them a motheaten or bumpy appearance.

4. The hind legs on the altered 3-leg are thick, and stocky looking.

5. The 3-leg has a series of lumps between the front and hind legs.

24

1937 D ALTERED TO 1937 D 3-LEG

ALTERED

6. The altered 3-leg does not have these lumps.
7. The beard tips of the 3-leg are narrow and pointed with the right tip longer.
8. The beard tips on the altered 1937 D are blunt and about even.
9. The hoof below the missing leg is a weak strike on the 3-leg.
10. The hoof is a strong strike on the altered; this is sometimes removed.

1924 P OR D DIME ALTERED TO 1921 P OR D

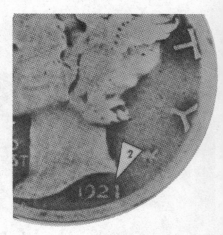

GENUINE   ALTERED

1. On the genuine 1921, the numbers in the date are of even thickness and evenly spaced.

2. The altered coin, the number "1" is spaced too far from the number "2." Examine for evidence of tampering around the last number "1."

Note the difference in style and position of numbers in date.

1934 D DIME ALTERED TO 1931 D

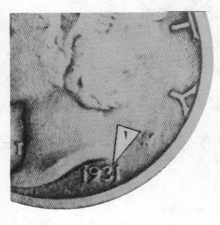

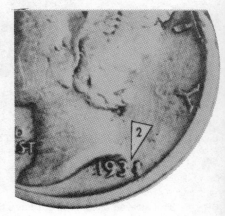

GENUINE   ALTERED

1. On the genuine 1931 D, the numbers in the date are evenly spaced.

2. On the altered 1934 D, the space between the "3" and the last "1" is too wide.

1942 DIME ALTERED TO 1942/41 DIME

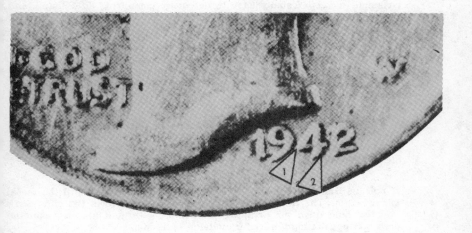

GENUINE

A 1942 dime is altered by soldering a "1" over the front of the "2."

On the genuine 42/41 the "4" in the date is doubled. This can be seen at the upper left (1) and lower right (2). The metal at the lower right is the tail of the second "4."

This coin also has been altered by the use of the acid treatment. The 4 is doubled and the 2 is painted on with asphalt paint. The coin is then relief-etched with the end result being a passable 42/41 coin.

ALTERED 1916 D DIMES

Altered 1916 D dimes have been made in the following ways:

1. 1916 S dime altered to 1916 D by shaving a blob "S" mint mark to resemble a "D." Usually easy to detect by comparing size, shape, and position of mint mark with a genuine or photo of a genuine coin.

2. A 1916 obverse hollowed out and "D" mint reverse inserted, or the other way around. This is very hard to detect if the size, shape, and position of the mint mark is like the genuine. Examine obverse and reverse next to the rim for the seam with a good glass. Compare mint mark position with a genuine.

3. A "D" mint mark is glued to a 1916 P coin. Examine the base of the mint mark for the seam. Beware of dark area around mint mark as this could hide the seam. Compare with genuine for mint mark position, size, etc. If it looks phoney treat mint mark with acetone.

4. A hole is drilled into the obverse opposite the mint mark until the metal is very thin. The thin metal is then punched up to form the mint mark and the hole filled in. Compare mint mark with genuine, also examine obverse opposite mint mark for evidence of filled hole.

5. A 1916 P obverse and a "D" mint reverse are planed down and soldered or glued together. Usually easy to detect as the reeded edge is fouled up or very unlike the reeding on a genuine if touched up.

6. The last number of a 1917D, 1918D, 1919D, or the third number of a 1926D is removed and replaced by a number making it a 1916D. Easy to detect by comparing position of numbers in date with a 1916 obverse and genuine reverse for mint mark, size, and position.

Examine the position of the D mint mark. Denver mint records indicate that there were four working dies used for the 1916D reverse; these are:

To be genuine the mint mark must match one of these positions exactly. If you have a suspect coin treat the mint mark area with acetone. If it is a glued mint mark it can be removed by pushing the mint mark a few minutes after treating with acetone. Examine for evidence of soldered mint marks.

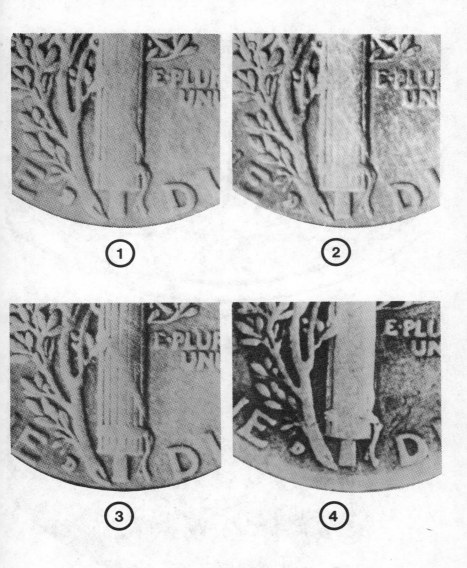

(1)

(2)

(3)

(4)

Examine the position of the D mint mark. Denver mint records indicate that there were four working dies used for the 1916D reverse; these are:

No. 1 — high tilts right.

No. 2 — high more vertical.

No. 3 — medium high.

No. 4 — low.

1917 TYPE 1 STANDING LIBERTY QUARTER ALTERED TO 1916 STANDING LIBERTY QUARTER

GENUINE

ALTERED

1. The fold of drape touches Liberty's foot and the bottom of the fold does not curve very much on the genuine 1916 quarter.

2. The fold of drape does not touch Liberty's foot on the altered 1917 T and the bottom of the fold is much more rounded than the 1916. This will also identify a dateless 1916 quarter.

1923 S STANDING LIBERTY QUARTER ALTERED FROM 1928 S

GENUINE   ALTERED

1. On a genuine 1923 S, the "3" has a flat top and the numbers are evenly spaced. The date is high, not recessed.

2. On an altered 1928 S, the "3" has a round top and is a little wide or spaced too far from the "2." The date is in a depression.

1932P QUARTER ALTERED TO 1932 D OR S MINT MARK SOLDERED OR GLUED TO PLAIN

ALTERED

1. Examine base of mint mark for a seam, a very thin line.

2. Compare size, position, and height of mint mark with a genuine. The mint mark should never be higher than the detail around it.

If you have a suspect coin treat the mint mark with acetone. If it is a glued mint mark it will fall off when you push it. Examine for evidence of removal of excess solder.

GENERAL INFORMATION ON SILVER DOLLARS

Alterations of the cent, nickel and the dime have been quite common for some time as these denominations are the most common and also the most wanted.

Altering silver dollars has increased in the past few years. The silver dollars listed in this section are but a few of the many coins that are altered.

On these larger pieces such as the silver dollar it is somewhat easier to detect some of the alterations which are quite a bit harder to find on the smaller pieces. This is due to the size of the field of the silver dollars.

Glue specks or solder joints or the imperfect fit of a transplanted mint mark can usually be spotted without the aid of a high powered glass.

Mint marks may appear to be more worn or to be newer than the rest of the coin if they have been transplanted from another coin.

Comparison of a questioned coin with genuine coins of the same date can sometimes show up variations which might go unnoticed.

Silver dollars have been altered by machining one part to fit inside another machined coin. This will make the ring of the coin very flat and dull.

A genuine obverse and reverse muled together are also becoming more popular. Silver dollars are good subjects for this activity due to the mint mark and date being on opposite sides of the coin. These coins will normally be a little smaller in diameter and will not have a true ring. The telltale seam between the two halves is difficult to camouflage as the match of the reeding is a problem. These coins reproduce a dull flat sound also.

Studying the major die varieties of the silver dollar series is a must for collectors of these coins. The collector of the key coins in the silver dollar series would have a running knowledge of varieties and how alterations are produced.

Added mint marks or deletion of mint marks can sometimes be determined by knowing the type of variety minted at each of the mint involved. All genuine coins will have a square base for all the lettering, dates and mint marks.

1892-S SILVER DOLLAR

Brilliant uncirculated or at least the uncirculated grade of the 1892 Philadelphia silver dollar are the only coins really worth the effort to alter to the 1892-S.

The addition of the S mint mark to the Philadelphia coin is all that is needed. Other known S coins have been used and two of them are the 1890-S and the 1891-S.

Mint mark variations of the San Francisco mint are broken down into four different types.

A small square S was used from 1878 to 1879.

A small rounded S was used from 1879 to 1900.

A much larger S was used from 1899 to 1904 with rounding at the top and the bottom of the letter.

A very small or micro S was used on the 1921 peace dollar.

Any of the mentioned mint marks will not have the squareness at the base of the mint mark where the mark has been transplanted.

SMALL ROUNDED S

LARGE OPEN S

1893-S SILVER DOLLAR

GENUINE

FLAT NUMBERS IN DATE

ROLLED RIM   **SMALL S**

1893-S SILVER DOLLAR

This date, 1893-S, is considered to be the most altered coin of any of the U.S. silver dollars. A great number of other dates have been used to make the 1893-S.

1893-P with the transplanted S mint mark is one of the methods. Be sure of the size of the S mint mark as outlined under the 1892-S coin. Check the area under the mint mark; look for traces of solder or glue on the field of the coin.

The 1898-S is often used for alteration by cutting or changing the last digit into a 3. The spacing will be excellent and the mint mark will be genuine but tool marks, abrasion or other tell tale features will be found in the date area. Electric erasers are often used to clean up the area around conversion methods such as cutting.

A recut 8 into a 3 normally will have two semi circles making the 3 while a genuine 3 will have a different shape inside the top of the digit.

1883-S is often used by transplanting a number 9 in place of the second 8. Squareness and ill fit to the coin field will give this alteration away.

Repunched date varieties have been recorded for the 1883 Philadelphia silver dollar production. Adding an S and making a transplanted 9 to a repunched 1883 date is a dead give away on the altered coin.

1894-P SILVER DOLLARS

Second in line for alteration is any coin that can be used to reproduce what appears to be an 1894 Philadelphia silver dollar.

The quickest and best method is to remove the mint mark from an 1894-O silver dollar.

However most New Orleans silver dollars in the later part of 1800 were light strikes. The breast feathers on the eagle will be light on the reverse of the coin. The obverse will also indicate the light strike by a wide flat hairline over the ear of the portrait.

The color of the silver dollars from New Orleans is a little different than the color of the alloys used by the other mints. They show a white silver cast rather than a chrome silver color as seen on the coins from San Francisco and Philadelphia.

The general grading of the New Orleans silver dollars is less than described in the Brown & Dunn Grading Guide, even for the uncirculated coins when they first came from the coining press.

Altered 1894-O coins for the 1894 Philadelphia mint can be detected with information about the New Orleans varieties, color of the alloy and the grading.

Light reflection from a hi-intensity lamp can be a big help in detecting the mint mark removal area. This can also be accomplished without the aid of magnification.

Look for tell tale marks of an electric eraser which could be used to polish up the field in the areas where marks have been removed and then used to blend the general area of the coin.

1895-S SILVER DOLLAR

Usually this one is made from an 1885-S coin. A transplanted 9 is used. The mint mark is the give away on this operation. The various sizes of mint marks used by the San Francisco mint indicates that a closed S was used on the 1885-S while the genuine 1895-S coin had a mint mark in which the S was more open.

The types of S mint marks are listed under the information about the 1892-S dollar.

1896-S SILVER DOLLAR

Quite a large number of these have been made from Philadelphia minted silver dollars for 1896 by the use of a transplanted S.

The rim size is the variable for the two mints. The San Francisco minted silver dollars carried a flatted and rounded rim. The 1896 Philadelphia silver dollar usually has a wire edge rim. With this in mind we find that a high wire edge rim with an S mint mark would tip the coin as one that was altered.

Transplanted mint marks are soldered, glued or plugged into the correct coin area. Plugged mint marks are mint marks removed from genuine coins and then have a plug attached. Holes are drilled into the coin to be altered and the plug is set into the area. This can normally be determined by examining the area on the opposite side of a suspected mint mark.

1899-CC SILVER DOLLAR

This is a simple case of obtaining an 1899 Philadelphia silver dollar and adding the CC mint mark. This can be done by acid etch, photoengraving, plugging or soldering.

Carson City used two basic size mint marks. The CC that appears on the 1878 and 1880 is the small mint mark, the same size mint mark they used on the seated liberty silver dollars.

The large CC was first used on the liberty head dollar in 1879.

Size of the mint mark used on the suspect coin could be food for further investigation.

The Philadelphia silver dollars for 1899 have a high wire rim on the obverse while the 1899 CC coins have a flat rim with almost no rim height.

An altered 1879 CC to an 1899 CC can also be detected by the size of the numerals in the date. The 1879 date is much larger than the 1899.

1901-P SILVER DOLLAR

This is normally a 1901-O with the mint mark removed if the piece is an altered coin.

Again this would be a light strike as the New Orleans coins of the latter part of 1800 and the early 1900 strikes were noted for this feature.

The color of the silver used in the New Orleans silver dollars had a different cast than the other mints. More silver is featured rather than the chrome silver color of the other mints.

Reflection of hi-intensity lamps will normally show up the area of the mint mark removal. The coin when held in the light and tilted at different angles will usually show up the area from which the mint mark was removed. This can be done without magnification.

1903-S SILVER DOLLAR

To make this coin it is usual to alter a 1903-P dollar by just adding the S mint mark. The S normally added is the closed S type as the open S is too difficult a letter to transplant and avoid detection.

There are some genuine 1903-S coins with the closed S but the rim again is the key to this problem. The S have the flat rim as compared to the wire edge of the Philadelphia silver dollars for 1903.

For the variations of the S mint mark see the information as listed under the 1892-S coin.

GENUINE COINS

**FLAT NUMERALS IN DATE
SMALL RIMS**

LARGE OPEN S

ROUNDED NUMERALS IN DATE

HIGH RIMS

37

1904-S SILVER DOLLAR

All 1904-S silver dollars should have the large S and not the small square S or the small rounded S.

The coin can be a 1900-S or the 1901-S altered to make the 1904-S. In either event the last digit will have to be deleted and a 4 transplanted.

Again this is a check under a hi-intensity lamp for the indications of the elimination of the 0 or the 1. Sometimes the conversion of the 1 to the 4 will take place but spacing is a factor involved with this operation. The end result will look squeezed. More than likely the 1 will be eliminated and a 4 transplanted.

1928-P SILVER DOLLAR

This coin can be made by removing the S from a 1928-S coin.

The rim of the Philadelphia coins for this particular year are flat while the San Francisco coins have the high wire effect.

The 1928-S peace dollars are usually poorly struck and removal of the mint mark to make the Philadelphia alteration degrades the coin.

1934-S SILVER DOLLAR

This one can be made by using a 1934-P silver dollar. Almost all of the S mint production for the peace dollars were poor strikes. This would indicate that much of the design is missing from the S coins which is a give away.

Generally the Philadelphia coins in the silver dollar peace series were sharp strikes with most of the detail.

The sharpness of the detail on any offered 1934-S silver dollar would be suspect that it had been altered.

GOLD

1911 2½ GOLD ALTERED TO 1911 D. To alter the 1911, a "D" is punched on the coin and the area around the mint mark is shaved away. Hold the coin at eye level and you will notice the depression on the altered coin. Also the mint mark will not be above or higher than the field. (See 1909 S VDB). On a genuine coin, the mint mark is raised above the field. Beware of split coins and soldered mint marks.

1909 D ALTERED TO 1909 O 5-DOLLAR GOLD PIECE. Examine the mint mark with a glass for evidence of tooling on upper left and lower left of mint mark.

1922 GRANT MEMORIAL HALF

WITHOUT STAR

WITH STAR

1922 GRANT MEMORIAL HALF WITH STAR OBVERSE ALTERED FROM GRANT WITHOUT STAR. A star is punched onto the no-star. Examine the reverse for a flat spot opposite the obverse star. To be genuine it must have the die break. An altered coin will show the flat spot on the reverse at a 3 o'clock position.

DETECTING COUNTERFEIT MINT ERRORS

Since the early 1960's, when the collecting of mint errors and oddities began to play a more important part in the general coin collecting hobby, there has been a steady increase in the number of collectors interested in coins that have been misstruck in one way or another. With the increasing interest has come higher and higher prices for some of the planchet and striking errors that are both scarce and in greatest demand.

Just as with the date and mint collector's coins, the high prices have attracted the criminal element, who have been profiting by altering genuine coins into fake mint errors, or even adding fake errors to genuine mint errors to increase their value.

With the sophisticated technical equipment available today, there have been instances already of complete dies being produced, especially by a group of counterfeiters on the west coast, who went into mass production in 1968 and 1969, producing fake strike cents, quarters and halves, as well as 1942/41 dimes.

Thousands of fake error coins were produced, especially fake 2nd strikes on genuine 1st strikes, and even the silver granules traded by the government for silver certificates were struck and sold as planchet fragments.

U. S. issue silver granule struck with counterfeit dies.

Ironically, at about the same time, the General Services Administration held a public auction of a quantity of used 1968-S proof dies that were used at San Francisco to produce the 1968 proof sets. The dies supposedly had been defaced with a welding torch, but they were snapped up and have since been appearing on the collector's market, offered with as much as "60% of the die surface undamaged." In early 1973 some of the products of these dies began showing up in offerings to collectors and dealers as fake 2nd strikes on business strike genuine 68-S nickels.

Two coins with fake second strikes from 1968-S proof dies. Under a lens, the original coins show circulation wear, contrasting markedly with the polished die 2nd strikes. Only a small portion of the die was needed to make the 2nd strike, and since the counterfeiter didn't have a matching reverse die, the coin was simply placed on the end of a machined rod. The same type of 2nd strike may show up with the proof like surface artificially toned. Both coins show evidence of being heated to soften them for the 2nd strike.

Just about every class of mint error can, and has been faked at one time or another in the brief history of error collecting. Besides the coins that have faked doubling from being rippled with a revolving wire brush, to the fake thin planchet error made by dipping a coin in acid, we also find coins with solder, glue or even globs of metal from a welding rod that have been added to imitate genuine mint errors. Both deliberate and accidental alteration of coins give many collectors problems in identifying genuine errors, so it is important that you study the error reference books on the market so that you can quickly detect the amateur fakes. The fake striking errors do require more knowledge and study, as in many cases they are of quite excellent workmanship.

In nearly all cases, the coins with fake errors produced on the west coast can be identified by the lack of collar marks, and many of the fake striking errors show signs that they were produced in a hydraulic press rather than in an impact press.

A fake error from the 1964 half dollar dies. The things to look for include:
1. *The letters in "Liberty" are abnormally elongated toward the rim.*
2. *The proof-like finish. Some versions will be found with artificial toning or wear.*
3. *Lack of collar marks. This manufacturer never successfully made a collar to go with the home made dies.*
4. *The B in Pluribus frequently, but not always looks like an 8.*
5. *Rays on reverse are often broken.*
6. *This is the die with the die crack thru the R in America, but carefully positioned so that that part of the die doesn't show on this strike.*

When a coin is struck outside the collar, as is the case for broadstrikes and off center strikes, it will usually be resting on top of the collar. If the collar is jammed, the coin will be driven down onto it by the upper die, and the edge of the collar will make an indentation in the coin along the edge of the portion struck by the die. Even if the collar is loose, the inertia of its mass will cause it to resist the downward movement of the coin enough so that markings will show on the coin. These semicircular indentations are parallel to the edge of the die strike, and close to it, especially prominent at the rims of a struck coin, or across the upset rim of a planchet. Care should be taken with any off center strike, double or multiple strike to make sure that the collar marks are present, usually with the reverse die.

The GSA also sold some collars along with the dies, so that it is very likely that any new production of fake errors will show collar marks. However, there are still hundreds of the old fakes that got into the hands of unwitting collectors, and fresh quantities of the previously made fakes are periodically moved into the market, so they will be continuing to show up for years to come, as the older collections are broken up or sold.

Only a few of the proof die strikes have shown up so far, apparently "testing" the market. Two of the coins examined were business strikes which had been in circulation before being struck a second time with the proof dies from the GSA sale, so it was quite noticeable that the 2nd strike was from a polished die. In addition, the edges of the 2nd strike showed evidence of being squeezed in a hydraulic press rather than an impact press. Both coins showed evidence of having been heated to anneal, or soften them.

When examining error coins for fake striking errors, it is important to look closely for evidence of heating, as it is nearly impossible to make a 2nd strike on a coin without annealing it.

Other points to look for when attempting to detect counterfeit or altered mint errors include artificial "wear" which may be done to cover the signs of changes made in the coin metal — a point which of course applies to alteration of the date or mint mark as well. Just as the maker of counterfeit currency will "age" the notes, so do coin counterfeiters abrade a fake, or cover it with grime to help hide what they've done to the coin.

Watch too for the cracked or broken planchet or coin that has been "helped" by inserting a sharp tool to widen a crack or split, or that has had pressure applied to break the planchet or coin in two.

In the case of the silver granules, and a number of fakes struck on staples or other pieces of junk, it is usually possible to detect the fake by the reaction of the metal at the edges of the struck object, which are rounded instead of showing at least a portion of the edge as rough or jagged as should be the case when striking an irregularly shaped object.

The same technique of hollowing out one coin and fitting a different obverse or reverse can be applied to fake rotated die errors, and should be closely watched for on the larger coins where the substantially higher value makes the extra effort to fake this error worthwhile.

With the increased interest in gold coins, as the price of gold shot up, there has also been an increase in the interest in gold coin errors, with some of the error values running into five figures. The response from the counterfeiters, perhaps the same fakers who have been busy duplicating gold coins for hundreds of years, was immediate, with fake off center strikes and multi-strikes showing up on the market at once. Several were quickly spotted by error experts, causing the counterfeiters to withdraw other "samples" from the market, but they will undoubtedly reappear.

The best defense against any counterfeiter is to know your dealer, buy only from a reputable dealer or a reputable collector, demand and get a money back guarantee, and get any coin of value authenticated while the guarantee is still in effect.

In the case of error coins, the best defense is accurate knowledge of the minting process, and some of the things that can go wrong that produce genuine error coins. For detailed information on error coins and the minting process, we recommend "The Official Variety and Oddity Guide to U.S. Coins"—6th Edition—by Alan Herbert, also distributed by ANCO, and available at most coin shops and hobby supply stores across the country.

To assist in combatting error coin counterfeiting, the three national mint error clubs have appointed authenticators to work with club members in determining whether their coins are genuine or not. For additional information, and charges for non-members, contact any of the following:

Alan Herbert—Authenticator for CONE and BIE Guild
Box C
Dept. DC
Deadwood, SD 57732

John Devine—Authenticator for CONE and NECA
P.O. Box 685
Dept. DC
Newbury Park, CA 91320

Duane Spellman—Authenticator for NECA
Box 147
Dept. DC
Simi, CA 93065

For both date and mint coins and error coins, the American Numismatic Association has set up their Certification Service. For information as to rates, contact:

Charles Hoskins, Director
ANA Certification Service
Box 87, Ben Franklin Station
Washington, DC 20044

In all cases, write first for mailing instructions from all of these authentication sources, before sending any coins, and include a stamped, self addressed envelope for a reply.

A counterfeit doubled die error. Error experts differ on this coin, one of a half dozen reported, and subsequently confiscated by the Secret Service. The author believes it to be counterfeit because there is no apparent difference between the amount of relief of the 1st and second impressions of the hub in the die, and thus on the struck coin both images appear the same size, without the tell tale tapering of the first image on the genuine doubled die.

A genuine multiple strike. Note that in this case each succeeding strike has mostly obliterated the preceding strike or strikes. This is almost always the case except for very recent dates—1972 and later. The Mint is now softening the planchets more, and using less pressure to strike the coins, so that the multiple strike often shows the previous strike clearly "under" the last strike.

A fake multiple strike error. The coin shows evidence of having been heated to soften it for the multiple impressions. Examine any such coin closely for discoloration.

A genuine broadstrike 1938–P dime. These occur when the collar (which forms the reeded edge of the coin) fails to come up around the blank as it is being struck by the dies, allowing the coin to spread out sideways, usually with a tapered edge.

A fake broadstrike error, probably produced in a hydraulic press rather than a coining press. Note the extremely wide unstruck rim, evidence that the metal was squeezed slowly, rather than being struck sharply by the dies.

A genuine 1972–P Doubled Die cent. Note that the 1st impression—the one on the left of each letter around the rim—is weaker and smaller than the 2nd impression. This is because the hub did not penetrate into the die as far on the 1st impression. Compare this genuine doubled die error with the counterfeit error on page 44.

Section 331 — Title 18, U. S. Code

Whoever fraudulently alters, defaces, mutilates, impairs, diminishes, falsifies, scales, or lightens any of the coins minted at the mints of the U. S., or any foreign coins which are by law made current or are in actual use or circulation as money within the U. S.; or "Whoever fraudulently possesses, passes, utters, publishes, sells, or attempts to pass, utter, publish, sell, or bring into the U. S. any such coin knowing the same to be altered, defaced, mutilated, impaired, diminished, falsified, scaled, or lightened — shall be fined not more than $2,000 or imprisoned not more than five years, or both."

The interpretation of the above statute recently made, takes the position that this section prohibits the alteration of dates or mint marks on U. S. coins for the purpose of defrauding coin collectors.

HOW TO DETECT COUNTERFEIT PAPER MONEY
Facts and techniques used in distinguishing authentic paper money from counterfeit.

IS IT PHONEY?
By
Chuck O'Donnell, N.L.G.

From ancient times the skillful art of counterfeiting has been man's attempt to "get something for nothing!" Today there are many fine examples of counterfeit coins of the second century before Christ. Down through the centuries we are constantly reminded that man continues to prey upon his fellow man. So serious was this crime, that until recent years, death was the penalty for those caught plying the trade. Many of our colonial and continental notes bore the announcement "death to the counterfeiter" or some similar advice. Yet despite the severity of the penalty there were those who were willing to take the chance.

Every single day the American public is victimized by counterfeit money and forged checks. Those who handle volumes of money must constantly be alert. The United States Secret Service cannot successfully reduce and prevent these crimes without the complete cooperation of the general public.

KNOW YOUR MONEY

In 1929 when the current or "small size money we now use was first issued, much planning had gone into making it the most reliable and secure paper money in the world. So that the public could easily recognize the genuine money, certain features of the currency were "standardized" and remain through all the years unchanged. The portrait on each denomination is always the same. George Washington on the $1.00 notes, Thomas Jefferson on the $2.00, Abraham Lincoln on the $5.00, Alexander Hamilton on the $10.00, Andrew Jackson on the $20.00, Ulysses Grant on the $50.00 and Benjamin Franklin on the $100.00. Denominations no longer printed include William McKinley on the $500.00, Grover Cleveland on the $1,000.00, James Madison on the $5,000.00, and Samuel Chase on the $10,000.00. The back or reverse side of our money also has standard features. The $1.00 note has the great seal of the U.S., the $2.00 has the "Signing of the Declaration of Independence", the $5.00 has the Lincoln Memorial, the $10.00 has the U.S. Treasury building, the $20.00 has the White House, the $50.00 has the U.S. Capitol and the $100.00 has the Independence Hall. With these standard features in mind, let us examine the photograph of the $20.00 Federal Reserve note (on next page).

CURRENCY TERMS

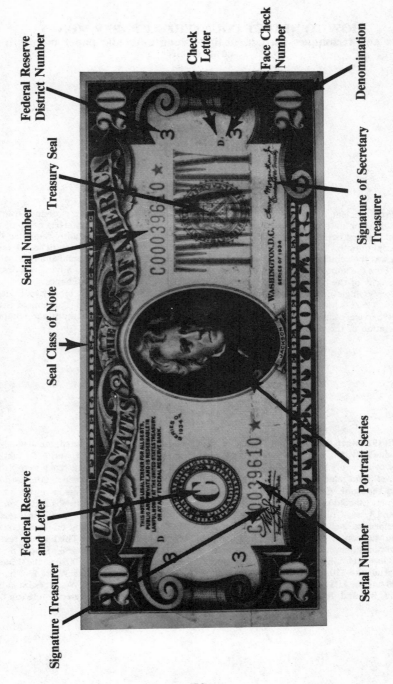

The "DENOMINATION" will appear in numerals in each of the four corners on both the face and back. The denomination is spelled out "twenty dollars" across the bottom on both the face and back.

The FEDERAL RESERVE SEAL and letter shown to the left of the portrait will be one of twelve Federal Reserve Districts into which the U.S. is divided:

1-A - Boston	5-E - Richmond	9-I - Minneapolis
2-B - New York	6-F Atlanta	10-J - Kansas City
3-C - Cleveland	8-H- St. Louis	12-L - San Francisco

Note that the letter corresponds to its numerical location in the alphabet, i.e. A-1, B-2 etc. Within the Federal Reserve seal you will find the district spelled out, the photo shows a note on the 3rd or "C", Philadelphia District. The Class of note is spelled out across the top of the note, in the photo it is Federal Reserve Note. Other currency also in circulation are the Silver Certificates and United States Notes. On very rare occasions one may see a Gold Certificate or a piece of National Currency. Each of these various classes of currency is distinguished by a different color Treasury Seal to the right of the portrait. The seal on Federal Reserve Notes is always green, on Silver Certificates it is blue, on United States Notes it is red, on National Currency it is brown and on Gold Certificates it is yellow.

The SERIAL NUMBER will appear twice on each note, in the upper right and in the lower left of the face of the note. The serial number, (except on National Currency), will always have eight digits, and prefix and suffix letters. The prefix letter will correspond with the letter in the seal. The Federal Reserve District number will appear in each of the four corners of the face. This number MUST match the letter in the seal, 1 for A, 2 for B, 3 for C etc. The suffix letter advances with each 100 million notes printed. Starting with suffix A, 100 million notes are printed with serials 00 000 001 thru 100,000,000. Since there are only eight numbering wheels, the 100 millionth note appears as 00 000 000 and is pulled out during the inspection and replaced by a "star" note. A star note is one that has been printed with an asterisk as the suffix and is used to replace damaged or spoiled notes in addition to replacing the 100 millionth note.

The SIGNATURES of the Secretary of the Treasury and the Treasurer of the United States appear to the right and left respectively of the face of the note.

The TREASURY SEAL appears to the right of the portrait. The face check letter and number appear to the lower right of the face. The check letter is repeated in the upper left of the note as part of the position number. The check number is a cross reference to the "plate" number which has been cut off when the notes were cut to circulating size. This enables the Bureau of Engraving and Printing to locate a defective printing plate when a run of notes are badly printed.

The SERIES is the way paper money is dated. Until Secretary of the Treasury Simon changed the policy for establishing the series, the year in which the Face design was approved became the series, as in the note pictured, 1934 represents a new face design. Whenever there was a change in either signature, a small letter was added to the year, thus a signature changes occur, the series would change to 1934A, 1934B, etc.

The PORTRAIT is the central design and the most prominent feature of our currency. In the upper left is the "position" of the note within the present 32 subject sheets being printed.

Imagine the sheet being divided into four parts. The upper left quadrant (or fourth part of the sheet is quadrant 1, the lower left is quadrant 2, the upper right is quadrant 3, and the lower right is quadrant 4.

Within each quadrant we find two rows of four notes each. From top to bottom the notes are identified as A, B, C, and D. The second row is E, F, G and H. Thus we find the extreme upper left note is in position A while the extreme lower right note would be in position H4. The letter corresponding to this position number is carried down to the face check in the lower right of the note. The sheets of notes are printed so that each serial number has a specific position in the sheet and those responsible for determining the authenticity of our currency know the formula to determine whether a serial number is in the right position or not. Additionally, each of these special features must be correct and in the right place, otherwise the note is either an error or a counterfeit.

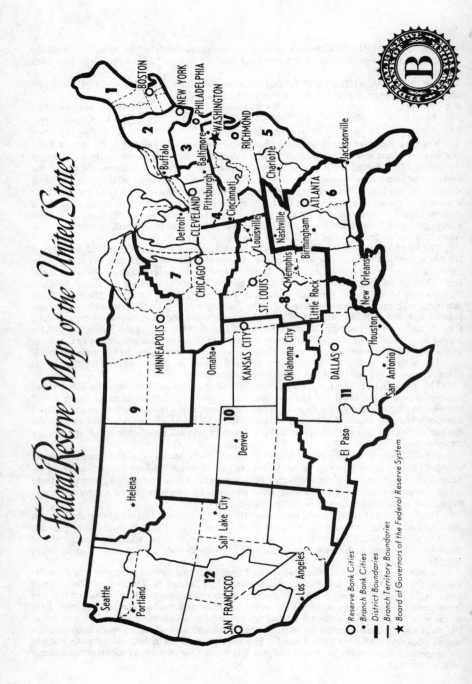

Federal Reserve Map of the United States

1
BOSTON
2
NEW YORK
Buffalo
3
PHILADELPHIA
Baltimore
WASHINGTON
Pittsburgh
RICHMOND
5
Cincinnati
Charlotte
Jacksonville
Detroit
CLEVELAND
4
Louisville
Nashville
ATLANTA
6
7
CHICAGO
St. LOUIS
8
Memphis
Birmingham
Little Rock
New Orleans
MINNEAPOLIS
Omaha
KANSAS CITY
Oklahoma City
Houston
9
10
Denver
DALLAS
San Antonio
El Paso
11
Helena
Salt Lake City
Seattle
Portland
12
SAN FRANCISCO
Los Angeles

O Reserve Bank Cities
• Branch Bank Cities
▬ District Boundaries
▬ Branch Territory Boundaries
★ Board of Governors of the Federal Reserve System

FIRST QUADRANT

A1 A00000001A A100	E1 A00080001A E100
B1 A00020001A B100	F1 A00100001A F100
C1 A00040001A C100	G1 A00120001A G100
D1 A00060001A D100	H1 A00140001A H100

SECOND QUADRANT

A2 A00160001A A100	E2 A00240001A E100
B2 A00180001A B100	F2 A00260001A F100
C2 A00200001A C100	G2 A00280001A G100
D2 A00220001A D100	H2 A00300001A H100

THIRD QUADRANT

A3 A00320001A A100	E3 A00400001A E100
B3 A00340001A B100	F3 A00420001A F100
C3 A00360001A C100	G3 A00440001A G100
D3 A00380001A D100	H3 A00460001A H100

FOURTH QUADRANT

A4 A00480001A A100	E4 A00560001A E100
B4 A00500001A B100	F4 A00580001A F100
C4 A00520001A C100	G4 A00600001A G100
D4 A00540001A D100	H4 A00620001A H100

HOW TO DETERMINE A COUNTERFEIT

Security or money printing in the United States is done by the intaglio method. This simply means that the printing plate has the design "cut" down into the plate. Ink is applied to the plate, then "wiped" off, leaving the ink down in the incised lines, and the surface of the plate clean. Paper is then placed over the plate and pressure applied so that the paper is forced down into the engraving and picks up the inked design. This accomplishes two things—first the process and equipment are so expensive that few counterfeiters are willing or able to use the method. Secondly, the force needed to push the paper down into the engraved lines creates a "third dimension" look, or depth to the impression, particularly "depth" which is impossible to accomplish by any other printing method. If the portrait appears "flat" or lifeless, it may well be suspected. All currency is printed, using security formula ink. Most counterfeit currency is reproduced photographically not using ink. This is the reason when one counts genuine currency the fingers become quite dirty or black from the ink. You could count photographs, or photographed money all day and leave with clean hands! Take a suspect note, rub it lightly against a white paper or piece of cloth. If the ink comes off, it is probably a good note.

If the above tests do not satisfy you, try the following: On genuine notes the portrait appears lifelike and stands out distinctly from the fine lines in the background. The hairlines are clean and crisp. On counterfeit the portrait is lifeless, the background is generally too dark. The hairlines are not even and distinct, the portrait seems to blend into the background.

The Treasury Seal to the right, must be the correct color. The saw-tooth points are even, clear and sharp. On counterfeits the points may appear blunt or broken off. On the border of genuine notes the finely engraved lines are continuous, clear and distinct. On counterfeits they are invariably broken or weak.

Authentic currency is QUALITY. It is printed by experts on expensive machinery, and quality paper. Steel plates that are produced by expert engravers leave clear, crisp lines. Counterfeits lack this quality. They usually are a product of poor workmanship with poor equipment. If produced from a plate, they are generally photomechanically made causing loss of detail. It is printed on inferior paper and just looks phoney!

If you take a suspect bill, try to remember the person giving it to you. Try to memorize as complete a description of that person as possible, how he looks, what he wears, if possible a license tag number, any name or address he gives. Consult your local bank or call the United States Secret Service. Do not try to pass the note along — remember it is a crime not only to make counterfeit — but to have it or to pass it.

HOW TO DETECT COUNTERFEIT GOLD COINS
Facts and techniques used in distinguishing authentic gold coins from counterfeit.

SOME NOTES ON THE DETECTION OF COUNTERFEIT GOLD COINS

Gold coins have in general been counterfeited with greater frequency because of their high intrinsic value and more recently due to the value of numismatic rarities.

Two basic principals that apply to all coins are worth remembering:

A. Each and every coin will bear the characteristics of the process by which it was made.

B. Every coin has 3 sides — *obverse, reverse* and the *edge.*

To simplify the detection of bogus gold coins two basic categories will be considered. The first group will be coins produced by casting methods. The tell-tale signs of casting products all come from the methods used in casting. Some basic casting characteristics are as follows:

Bubbles
Air entrapped in the casting material or the mold material will produce a bubbled service.

Mold Texture
The texture of the molding material may be seen on the surface of the coin. Texture will vary from rough to almost non-existent.

Mold Flaws
Scratches, digs, chips and other imperfections in a mold will be transferred to the coin produced.

Process Characteristics
Traces of the casting process may be left on the coin. These can include:

RISER: The waste metal standing up through the gate of the mold when the mold is broken away from the cooled counterfeit coin.

FIN: The result of molten metal flowing into a crack in the mold during the casting process.

MOLD SCRATCH: A raised line on the surface of a cast coin as a result of a scratch on the surface of the mold.

MOLDING PIT: A depression in the surface of a cast coin as a result of excess foreign material in the mold.

Size Variance
Hot metals shrink while cooling, thus a cast coin will shrink in diameter and thickness from a genuine piece. Diameter comparisons may indicate a problem but should not be the sole criteria for judging a coin.

Edge Problems
Edge devices will often hide tell-tale signs of the casting process. Texture in the reeding may not be natural. Most coins struck in a collar will show drag lines created when the coin in ejected from the collar. Cast coins may be forced through a collar to produce drag lines. Frequently, a cast coin will shrink enough to pick up only partial drag traces when forced through a collar. The resulting edge will have drag lines on the ridges and a cast texture in the grooves.

The second group of counterfeits to be considered are coins struck from counterfeit dies. Die struck counterfeits present the greatest problems in the numismatic market place today. High quality reproductions made with precision and care may baffle the collector but are not impossible to detect. Again remember that a coin will bear characteristics of the process by which it is made. Most of the tell-tale signs of a counterfeit will be a result of the way the counterfeit die was produced. These small imperfections are "fingerprints" of the counterfeit die. The following "fingerprints" are some of the more commonly found counterfeit die imperfections:

Depressions
A counterfeit die that is made from a genuine coin will have the bag marks from the genuine coin as raised bumps on the die. If these bumps are not removed they will transfer to the coins as "depressions."

Tooling Marks
Corrections made to a counterfeit die with a small tool will leave marks on the die and thus marks on the counterfeit coins produced. Since tooling marks on a die are scratched into the die metal they appear as raised marks on the coins produced.

Additional characteristics of counterfeit die-struck coins can be any or all of the following:
Mis-matched Dies
Combinations of obverse and reverse that never existed.

Incorrect Edge Devices
Such as lettered edges when the correct edge is needed.

Multiple Matched Dies
Frequently counterfeit coins of different dates will bear the same reverse or obverse.

Whenever a coin is examined do not forget the second basic principle of examination. *Every coin has 3 sides: obverse, reverse,* and the *edge.* Check all 3 sides being sure to rotate the coin with relation to the source of light you are using. Microscopic examination is preferable but a well trained eye and hand glass are often sufficient.

A visual check may reveal some condemning points, but a physical check is also valuable.

Gold has traditionally been the standard of monetary exchanges throughout history. Reigning monarchs and elected governments have always taken great pride and care with their nation's gold coinage. As a result, the physical standards of gold coinage have generally been very high. The physical quality and standards of gold coins cannot be overlooked.

The gold content measured by specific gravity can be critical as well as the dry weight, diameter and thickness of a coin. A comparison with published national standards may reveal gross physical discrepancies that will not be notable from a visual examination.

Last but far from least importance is basic knowledge of the coin series with which you are dealing. Research by collectors and scholars also gives valuable information.

Professional opinions can be obtained from the American Numismatic Association Certification Service:

ANACS
818 North Cascade
Colorado Springs, CO 80903
(303) 473-9142

Extremely valuable bulletins on counterfeits are published by the International Bureau for the Supression of Counterfeit Coins:

IBSCC
P. O. Box 4QN
London, W1A 4QN
England

**1855
ONE DOLLAR WITH SMALL
LIBERTY — WORTH $1500.00**

**1825
TWO AND ONE HALF
DOLLAR UNDRAPED
WITH ROUND CAP
WORTH $7500.00**

**1879
FOUR DOLLAR WITH COILED
HAIR — WORTH $85,000.00**

**1873
FIVE DOLLAR WITH
CORONET — WORTH $3500.00**

1907
TEN DOLLAR
WORTH $700.00

1873
TWENTY DOLLAR
WITH LIBERTY HEAD
WORTH $600.00

**1907
MCMVII TWENTY DOLLAR
(ST. GAUDENS)
EX. HIGH RELIEF
WITH LETTERED EDGE
WORTH $235,000.00**

**1923
TWENTY DOLLAR
(ST. GAUDENS) WITH MOTTO
WORTH $500.00**

NEW RELEASE
THE ALL NEW — OFFICIAL 1979
"BLACKBOOK" PRICE GUIDES

"the world's largest selling price guide of its kind!"

PAPER MONEY $1.95

- covering U.S. currency - 1861 to date
- over 6200 buying and selling prices
- comprehensive grading section
- includes - Mules - Freaks - Errors Fractional and National currency
- Federal Reserve District information
- Functional inventory check list
- fully illustrated

COINS $1.95

- covering U.S. coinage - 1616 to date
- over 16,000 buying and selling prices
- computerized, up-to-date prices
- **NEW - EXPANDED A.N.A. GRADING SYSTEM**
- gold and silver coin value chart
- detecting altered coins section
- functional inventory checklist
- fully illustrated

STAMPS $1.95

- covering U.S. stamps - 1847 to date
- over 15,000 buying and selling prices
- **NEW - EXCLUSIVE GRADING SECTION**
- **FEATURING A FAST - FIND PHOTO INDEX**
- **OFFICIAL SCOTT NUMBERING SYSTEM**
- includes - General Issues - Mint Sheets U.N. Issues - Airmails - First Day Covers
- Functional inventory check list

BUY IT ● USE IT ● BECOME AN EXPERT

- Complete Reference Handbooks ● Fully Illustrated ● Accurate Pricing
- Keeping up with the expanding market in collectibles is our business

Send For Our New Catalog

CONTACT YOUR LOCAL BOOKSELLER OR

House of
Collectibles

"Exclusive Publishers of Official Price Guides"

771 Kirkman Road, Suite 100, Orlando, Florida 32811
Phone (305) 299-9343

Please send: _____ Coin Guide _____ Stamp Guide _____ Paper Money Guide   Total $_____
Please send a catalog of your complete line of collectible price guides

NAME _____ Apt. No. _____
                              (please print)
ADDRESS _____
CITY _____ STATE _____ ZIP _____

— NEW RELEASE —

THE OFFICIAL PRICE GUIDE TO
MINT ERRORS
AND
VARIETIES

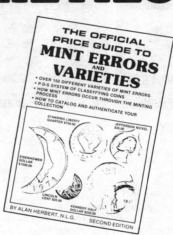

$3.95
SECOND EDITION

- The official system of cataloging and identifying the 150 different classes of mint errors, developed by Mr. Herbert, is the standard accepted by the majority of collectors in the numismatic world
- Each listed mint error classification is fully illustrated and detailed to explain the Plancet-Die-Striking System of identification
- Step-by-step, pictorial information on how coins are minted at the 3 U.S. mints and how mint errors occur
- Helpful hints on how you can set up your own system of cataloging and identifying your mint errors

House of Collectibles

CONTACT YOUR LOCAL BOOKSELLER OR —